# God is STRETCHING

Joseph Dean IV

# DEDICATION

This book is dedicated to my entire family, Lighthouse Ministries (LHM), St. Paul Baptist Church (STPBC) and Lighthouse International Fellowship (LIF).  Thanks for the push and growth.

# CONTENTS

In this book Joseph Dean teaches us how there is much in us that we are yet to experience. God wants to stretch us beyond what we believe we are capable of achieving. Growth, from a Kingdom perspective, takes place from the inside out. When we ask God for more, we must go through the process of stretching and expanding into areas that can make us uncomfortable.  Dean gives us an important key to the process, and that is our obedience to the Word of God. I was especially challenged by the fact that my obedience to God can also propel someone in my sphere of influence to their next level of blessing. Dean states that, "when God stretches you, he also moves you." Stretching is an uncomfortable process and requires us to remove the old stakes so that our tents are in position for enlargement.

After reading this book you will gain insights about how when God is stretching you, your obedience, and your integrity. He is positioning you for promotion. Stay in the process and run the race set before you. Know that when you are being stretched, it is not always the devil. When you allow God to stretch you, you have more to offer to the Kingdom of God.


Bishop Anthony T. Pettway, Sr.
Senior Pastor, Eastgate Bible Church

In *God is Stretching*, Joseph Dean forces us to take a good look at *why* we go through certain situations. Is it really the enemy? Or is it the preparation for a prayer to be answered? Have we considered that what we asked for requires a certain maturity that God is now *stretching* us into? After reading this book, I was confronted with my own experiences, as I recalled growth opportunities that I mislabeled as an attack from the enemy.

How challenging it is to be stretched by God?! The process can be painful, but it is necessary for our growth, maturity, and elevation. This book paints a beautiful picture of what God wants to stretch in us, some ways He stretches, and the reward of it all! When we realize that the process is not to hurt us but to promote us, we can go through the stretching with less hesitation and resistance.

Be encouraged as you turn each page! Apply these Kingdom principles and watch God's Word manifest in your life. Take this guided tour and allow God to *stretch* you into the person He created you to be!


Maryum Haston
Owner and Founder of Speak LIFE LLC

## ACKNOWLEDGMENTS

I am truly grateful to GOD for the opportunity to share with YOU what HE has given me.  I have been put in many situations that have STRETCHED me beyond what I have ever thought.  I realize that GOD wants me to reach my full capacity.  I hope that this book will help you better understand some of the pressure that is associated with life.

LHM, LIF and STPBC we have been stretched and pulled but we have stood the test and yes, we have grown.  Schmieka, once again you are truly a blessing and a class act. To my entire family, thank you for your steadfast support.

How could I pull all this off without you, Maryum Haston?  I don't have the words to express my gratitude for the press and momentum that you have brought to this area of my life.  Schmieka Dean, Laronda Raines and Ashley Dean thank you for proofreading and your editorial helps.

I don't have a magic word, but I do have a word that God has put in my Spirit for the body of Christ. There is a Kingdom sound! The sound is something that is released through the people of God.

Have you ever wondered why you felt exhausted and drained from life's pressure? Questioned if God has forgotten you or neglected your expressed concerns toward Him. This book will aid in giving you a better understanding of what stretching by God is and does. Often times we pray for increases in our lives, finances, and spiritual growth, not realizing the causes and effects those prayers place on our lives. When being stretched, we feel just that; at the brink of tearing and breaking but still standing. God Is Stretching, gives us the breakdown of the processes we encounter through the progression of where God is taking us.

When being stretched, it doesn't always feel good or look good. However, God wants to grow you up in the spirit! If you just continue pressing, the Holy Spirit will lift you up and walk you through the pressure of what appears to be a rough time in your life and walk with Christ. Once the journey is complete, and the storm is over, you'll realize that you're actually walking into victory. You stood the test of time! What God wants you to understand is that when the pressure is on you, the Holy Spirit is fighting and pulling you out!

*God Is Stretching*, highlights five areas in which God is stretching our lives. Not only does it highlight these much-needed portions of our lives, but it also gives us reference builders to apply daily. Remember these key points; in whatever you're doing obey what Gods says and wants you to do! No matter how it seems or appears trust the process. What God is doing WILL work for your good! This book will help you understand how God wants to mature us through stretching us beyond what we think our limits are, while providing reinforcements to apply while waiting on God.

Do you remember the elastic man from the cartoon Fantastic 4? His arms would get long, and he could stretch out his legs. His whole body could stretch!

God says that there are things inside of you that have not been tapped into! There are things that are lying dormant inside you that have not been used yet!

**God wants you to be reminded that He is stretching you!**

Background Scripture: Isaiah 54: 2-3 KJV

2 Enlarge the place of thy tent, and let them stretch forth the curtains of thine habitations: spare not, lengthen thy cords, and strengthen thy stakes;

3 For thou shalt break forth on the right hand and on the left; and thy seed shall inherit the Gentiles, and make the desolate cities to be inhabited.

Consider a balloon that has yet to be blown up, it represents your life. Then you start writing on that balloon, "give me more God"! It will be hard for you to fit all of that on the deflated balloon. This is what you have been asking God to do! To give you more in a small place. In the place that you are in, you have been saying, "God give me more; God I want and need more of You!"

You may say, "I need You to come in and move in my finances." He allowed you to be broke for a moment and you say, "I need more God!" But every time He gave you more, you really didn't want the more! You said you want to be a gift and He sends somebody to you, and you don't want to help them!

Now you weren't able to really write "give me more God" on the deflated balloon. But when you blow in the balloon, it stretches, and you are able to fit the words on it better. When the Holy Spirit begins to blow us up on the inside; every time He blows you up, He stretches you! This blow up, this stretching, doesn't feel good!

But you keep saying, "God I want more", and then you start clowning. You say, "God I want Your glory," then He allows all hell to break loose in your family. He breathes on you and on the inside of you, and you keep saying, "God I have to have more of You." The problem is you only want more and stay as the deflated balloon. God is saying, "you keep telling Me you want more of My glory", You want more of the weight, so He keeps blowing on you and inflating you, inflating the balloon because He knows how much pressure to apply to your life!

On the balloon that has been blown up you can write, "I want more glory" because there is room for it all to fit. You can say I want more love because now it fits. If you tried to write all of this on the deflated balloon, it won't fit! But because God applied pressure to you and breathed on and in you, you are able to fit more than when you were just a deflated balloon.

You say you want more patience, then your children start getting on your nerves. Yet you keep asking God for more patience. Well, how can you get more patience to fit on the deflated balloon?! God says you asked for more patience so I'm going to stretch you! He allows your children to get on your nerves because that is the process He uses to stretch you into gaining more patience! You really don't want to be bothered but you said you wanted more patience, so He allows something or someone to aggravate you!

You said you wanted more, but you really don't like people and you really don't even like to talk. Now you keep seeing folks around you pulling on you, calling your name and telling you to do something. Every time they pull you, God blows on you, inflating the balloon, making more out of you, giving you everything you need! He is blowing you up, making you bigger! You have all kinds of patience now. When you used to want to curse, you don't curse anymore. When you used to want to go off on folks, He bridles your tongue. You realize every battle, you don't have to fight or win; God will fight all of your battles! He knows how much you can handle and bear!

You are going to be in a season where God is going to make everything uncomfortable.  He is going to make it so uncomfortable, there will be so much pressure in your lives, but He is stretching you to make you a better person!

# *God is causing you to do things you never wanted to do!*

You all are trying to refuse what He is doing! This pressure is NOT the enemy it is God working FOR you. Some of you are trying to rebuke the enemy and this is God's business working on His behalf! You're on your knees saying you rebuke the devil and it's not the devil, it's God that willed this! You're saying you can't go through this anymore, and God is saying He is just stretching you!

It doesn't always feel good, it won't always look good, but God wants to grow you up in the spirit! If you just keep on pressing, the Holy Spirit will lift you up and walk you THROUGH the pressure. Then you will realize you are walking into victory! What God wants you to understand is that when the pressure is on you, the Holy Spirit will fight for you and pull you out!  And because the Holy Spirit is pulling you out you will walk into victory!

Some of you will just sit down and complain. You have given up and you're mad at God. God is saying all He was doing was stretching and developing you! You don't want to be developed! How many have said, "God I want more of You," and when you said that all hell broke loose? When you told Him you wanted to live for Him, everything started shutting down! And then you sat down on Him!

He says that with every stretch, there is movement! Every time God stretches you; He moves you! You feel the pressure because God wants to move you!

Let's say you have a tent. You have four stakes that are holding the tent down, but because God has stretched you, He begins to enlarge your territory. You must take the stakes up and move the tent out to make room for what God is going to do! The tent is getting bigger because God is stretching you to make room for the new things He is about to do.

Some of you won't move from the old place to the new place, so He applies pressure to you. In order to be enlarged and moved, you are going to be stretched beyond the point that you believed you could be stretched to!  Every time God gives you a moment to minister, don't miss it anymore, because you don't know what God wants to do in that moment for you!

There will be so much pressure on you, like the balloon, but you will **NOT** break because He says you were built for it!

So, you prayed and said, "Lord give me more joy, more peace, more strength!" Have you ever prayed that before? For more perseverance, more endurance; I want to be more productive in my life. But you don't want to go thought the process. You want these things, but you don't want to be stretched!

If you want an increase in your blessings, get ready for an increase of your testing! Sometimes you must be tried and proved! They are related to one another. I want to encourage you; don't give up! Don't quit! The pressing, the spiritual process, is all His way!

## *God is maturing you!*

God has purpose for everything He does! Some of the things you're going through is not the devil, it is God stretching you! Take confidence in knowing that He will strengthen you!

We pray we want more power. So, God says He has to make you bigger to give you more power and the process to get bigger is to go through a test. Be stretched even in your obedience to Him! If God sends you a word by somebody, if you know it's God you better act on it! You can't say the circumstances weren't right! Even in your obedience, He is stretching you now to obey!

God will pull and press you until it hurts. Until you say I have to get it right! In the middle of the stretching you tell God you have to stop, but then God will send you some encouragement! You will say you want more of God but when He puts you in the process, you want to walk out of it! You've been praying all this time and telling God you want Him to move on your behalf, but when He puts you in the process you want to give up!

## *Don't throw the towel in!*

Have you ever had to do something that you never thought you would do? Some of us are complaining about the process. You love God, but you're mad, and God wants to stretch your faith!

Background Scripture: Hebrews 11: 6 KJV

> [6]But without faith it is impossible to please him: for he that cometh to God must believe that he is, and that he is a rewarder of them that diligently seek him.

Faith is absolutely ESSENTIAL to your experience! We enter our whole relationship with God through faith. God may want you to do something that you have never done before, to stretch your faith!

He may want you to stop doing something you are doing. He may say, "sit down for a minute and get yourself together." He may want you to give something. He may just want you to say something to somebody or He wants you to stop saying stuff! He may want you to sell something and give the money to somebody. To start something or to end something. There are ministries that may not be in the church!

God wants us, by faith, to just love someone!  God is stretching us! Sometimes stretching means more responsibilities. He will give you assignments that you thought you couldn't do and then you see that you can do it! Will you obey and just do what you have been asked to do?!  Do you feel the pressure of the stretch? Do you want to walk out the stretch? Then I want to encourage you now to stay in the press!

This is a season of great stretching, of being uncomfortable. But in the midst of being uncomfortable, God is moving us. With every expansion there is movement! and God is going to stretch us in our obedience.

We need to understand obedience; it is an essential part of our Christian faith! Even Jesus was obedient unto death (ref Philippians 2:8). When I looked up the definition of obedience, it is defined as dutiful. When we are obedient to God, we become dutiful to Him! We all struggle with obedience because, if we're honest, sometimes we just don't want to obey, because it does not always feel good. It's not always popular when God tells you to do a thing and you don't want to do it!

*But God said to me, even obedience will submit to authority. When we obey God, we submit to His authority!*

As I was going to work one Wednesday, I walked to the door, then I got to the car, and the Lord said walk around your house and pray before you leave. Well, it's almost 8 o'clock and I'm saying God you want me to pray? I'm already late for work, if I pray, I'm going to be SUPER late! I'm just being honest! I said I can pray in the car on my way to work. I went back to the house, then back to the car. I did that about two times. I got in the car, the car is on and the Spirit says get out of the car, walk around your house and pray!

Now I don't argue back and forth with God, so I get out and I start praying. I hit the garage. I'm walking up the driveway, I'm turning to go by the front door and I'm praying. I keep walking and praying, and I walk into a huge puddle of water. A pipe had burst! Now I'm sure people saw me because my hands are lifted and I'm praising, realizing if I hadn't walked around the house like God said walk, I would have missed it!

Yes, I had a busted pipe, but I was so excited because I'm assuming it had just burst. I said God, if I had not been obedient, I would have missed Your warning and that busted pipe would have been worse than what it was!

How many times has God told us to do something and we didn't do it?! When God told you to serve and you wouldn't, you said no. God may tell you to give somebody something and you questioned it. God says, in this season of great stretching, He was going to stretch our obedience! In other words, He wants us to do what He tells us to do!

He told Jonah what to do; he didn't always obey. Because of his disobedience, he caused the other people on that ship to have a little chaos. Sometimes when we don't obey, we cause problems for folks around us; you can cause chaos for the people around you.

Remember when He told Noah to build the ark? There are times God will tell you to do some things that are not familiar to your spirit. They're strange and don't make much sense and you're asking God why! But we've got to obey Him!

## *Obey what God wants you to do!*

We're in a season where God is pushing and pulling us to get us to where we must go. Somebody's deliverance is tied in your words, and because you won't open up your mouth, their deliverance is still tied down! You're the hope somebody has been looking for. I know our hope is in Jesus, but I believe that we are God's hands and feet. We are the bodies moving around that He sends to encourage people. I often say we are the only Bible that some people read, so obey what God wants you to do!

There are some things that God will tell you to do that will not feel comfortable to your flesh. You're not going to want to do it. Let me help you out! God will give us rest when we need rest, but God is calling us outside the doors of the church to touch lives!

God is saying "can I use you?!" Will you make yourself available to Him? We're always singing "Lord I'm available to You" and falling out on Him. Will you just obey Him?! When He asks you to speak, will you speak for Him? If He asks you to be quiet, He needs you to be quiet. If He asks you to go, then go. And if He asks you to stay, stay.

Can you obey what He wants you to do, or do you have to wager with God asking is it really Him? If this is You God, then do this. Then God does it, then you say it again, God if this is You then do this. God is saying those days are over! He needs you to know His voice and move NOW! He says, My sheep know My voice! If you are of His sheepfold, you know His voice and when He speaks, He needs you to move!

## *Obedience is a big part of your worship*

I'm so excited because when you are obedient to God, you submit to His authority.  Some of us say we really trust God, but we only trust Him when we can see Him. Outside of what we see with our natural eye, we really don't trust God for real!

But God is saying, "I need you to trust Me and obey what I'm telling you to do"! I know it's uncomfortable, but this is a season of great stretching and movement! If He is going to stretch you, He is going to expand you! It may not feel good in the beginning, but when the end comes, it will be alright!

God showed me that this is a season of obedience and righteous connections. A season of great networking. You need somebody, you can't do this by yourself! If you think in this season you're going to walk it by yourself, you've already lost it!

You may say, "I don't like to call and ask folks for nothing", you've already lost it. You're already defeated because you can't do this by yourself! Drop your pride and your arrogance, pick the phone up, text or call, however you do it, and say I NEED your help right now in this season!

It may just be a conversation, a good word, a smile, a hug but God says in this season of righteous connections you can't walk by yourself. There may not be 15 people around you, there may only be 2 people holding you up in this season.  Superheroes in ministry is over! One man shows in ministry are over now, it takes the WHOLE body to work this out!

 I'm going to challenge you; will you obey Him? Can you tell God it's not about me, it's not about how I want to do it, but it's whatever You want me to do? God is asking, will you trust Him in this season?! Will you obey Him? This is a season of great obedience, no matter how foolish it may sound to your natural mind, if God tells you to do it, then just do it!

  God can give somebody a word to tell you that can save your whole house, but because you are so prideful, because the conditions aren't right when you get it, you sit on it! Can you obey? WILL you obey?! If God tells you to move and it's just for a season will you do it?

 God is doing some things that we don't even understand. It is only by the help of the Lord that we move, not because we've been so good, or that we always get it right, but it is by the grace of God that we are here now! That we are standing! What a mighty God we serve!

# 6 GOD IS STRETCHING YOUR CHARACTER

God is stretching the body of Christ!  We've talked about **God is STRETCHING "You".**  God is going to pull you into places that you didn't know you were going. It felt like you wanted to give up, but you couldn't give up, because He is going to keep pulling you and pulling you. God has assured us that we will not fail in this season!

Then we saw how **God is STRETCHING "Our Obedience"**. I talked about how one morning God instructed me to walk around my house. I was late for work, but the Spirit said walk around your house. When I walked around my house there was a mud puddle because there was a big leak in my house. I lifted my hands and I told God thank You anyhow! Why? Because if I had been disobedient, I would have missed the leak and it would have cost me more money and more damage.

Now we are going to talk about how **God is STRETCHING "Your Character"**. I asked God to take me through the scriptures!

Background Scripture: Romans 5: 3-5 NIV

> [3]Not only so, but we also glory in our sufferings, because we know that suffering produces perseverance; [4]perseverance, character; and character, hope. [5]And hope does not put us to

shame, because God's love has been poured out into our hearts through the Holy Spirit, who has been given to us.

In my preparation, I had to look up character. I had to find out what it really means. Character is a feature or a trait that forms the individual nature of one person or some things. Such qualities as honesty and integrity. There is a quality that God is trying to stretch out of you!

I almost had a wreck one day. A black Tahoe almost ran me off the road. I drove a little further and saw it run someone else off the road. As a believer, how do you respond? My old man would have gotten road rage and probably would have cursed him out! But the Lord said, how do you handle this now?

There was nobody in the car but me and my wife so if I would have cursed, no one would have heard me, but character had to step in! God told me, what you do when nobody is looking at you, is what really matters! Have you ever had road rage? I know I'm not the only one! Sometimes we get upset and the wrong things come out of our mouths! Sometimes we get upset and we do the wrong things!

So, God told me to ask you, the believers, how do you respond in these types of situations? Because when the praise team is singing, we can lift our hands and give God the glory! But when you're by yourself, can you STILL give God the glory?

We must learn how to be consistent in this season. God is stretching us to develop into the people that HE wants us to be. God has put you in situations to test your patience. He is sitting you in the midst of folks to see how you are going to respond. Can you still lift your hands in praise when the boss tells you you're not doing a good job? Can you still tell God thank you?!

God is stretching us in our *response!* How are you going to handle it now since you say you love God? There are a lot of saved people with some sharp tongues. There are a lot of saved people you can't ask any questions because if you ask, they will get offended!

God is stretching us in our *facial expressions!* You don't have to say anything, it's how you look! That's a part of your response.

God is stretching how we *interact with people!* Some of us don't have good interaction skills. But in this season, God is going to stretch you to a place, He's not going to break you, but HE wants to stretch you. He wants to stretch you to get the glory out of EVERYTHING you do! How you handle people, how you talk to people, when you're by yourself. He wants to get the glory. How you are with your significant other. Can God still get the glory out of what you're trying to do?!

A lot of us have our hands lifted up in the sanctuary, but at home, we're somebody else. On the job and in the vehicle, we are somebody else. Those same folks that said God do it, talk differently when they're not in church.

Verse 4 says, before you get character you have to learn perseverance. You have to know how to suffer! You have to go through something! You have to be rejected, lied on, talked about. You have to go through all of that just so perseverance can come.

Some think when you give God your hand it would be all roses, but this is when people really start walking away from you, when your family start turning on you. The ride or dies aren't ride or dies anymore, because you are saying God is a good God!

I wanted to I look up perseverance. Google describes it as a persistent action or course, a purpose, a state, in spite of guilt obstacles or discouragement. In other words, in spite of what I'm going through, I'm going to keep going!

Some of you can't go through anything! People can tell you are going through something by how you act. You must learn how to go through with hands lifted up! You must learn how to go through when there is no money in your account, hands lifted up, and say God do it anyway! I gave my tithes and I have faith that You will open up the windows of heaven and pour me out blessings that I don't have room to receive. I don't have it in my account, but I believe you're going to do it God! I don't know how you're going to do it and it's not for me to worry about it, but it's for me to trust You and walk through it!

There is a thing called slander! You can find yourself in court based on your feelings. Your character is building, and you have to know how to handle things according to the word of God!

A lot of us don't know how to handle things according to the word of God. It takes us out of our character. Every reaction that you have, you don't have to say it! Because you feel it in your heart, don't let it come out your lips. When you let it come out your lips, do you realize your lips, your words, frames your world? So, what comes from your tongue starts to happen!

How is the body of Christ going to respond? We are in the season where the church has to respond in a godly way! The church has to know how to respond! The enemy wants to be able to say, "I thought you were a preacher", or "I thought you were saved. I thought you loved God" so your responses are important!

Sometimes saying nothing is the best thing to do! Sometimes you have to go gather your thoughts and say, "God talk to me, so that I may respond to them!" Ask God to give you guidance, because you have to represent Christ!

How do you represent Christ? Don't get all uppity, because some of the ways you think you represent Christ are not really good. Go and ask your friend and your friend's friend how you really look! Understand, you need ONE friend that's not scared of you! The one that will tell you when you're acting a fool when something isn't godly.

Realize that you have to go through something for character to come out. Trials and tribulations will produce character. Character isn't being produced when everything around you is going good, or when you have a lot of money. But when you don't have it, how do you respond to it then? When all you have is 10 dollars in your account and God says give 5 away. Will you do it? You can give 5 away when you have 500, but when you don't have anything, how do you respond? What do you do?

Background Scripture: James 5: 2-8 NIV

> [2] Consider it pure joy, my brothers and sisters, whenever you face trials of many kinds, [3] because you know that the testing of your faith produces perseverance. [4] Let perseverance finish its work so that you may be mature and complete, not lacking anything. [5] If any of you lacks wisdom, you should ask God, who gives generously to all without finding fault, and it will be given to you. [6] But when you ask, you must believe and not doubt, because the one who doubts is like a wave of the sea, blown and tossed by the wind. [7] That person should not expect to receive anything from the Lord. [8] Such a person is double-minded and unstable in all they do.

You have to let patience do what it has to do! Some of you want to jump out of the process, and when you jump out of the process, you stop maturing!

You're mad because of the process but the reason you're in the process is so that God can mature you. You're mad about the wrong thing! God has you in the process to develop you, and you are all bitter and bent out of shape. You won't get excited about it but you must stay in the process.

## *Learn to lift your hands in the process and see how God shifts it!*

People would rather mope and complain about it. They're in a shell, all depressed. But if you lift your hands up in the middle of the process. You talk about praise confuses the enemy. Confuse your enemy then! Break out in a praise! When I get tired of going through, I shift the atmosphere myself! I can give a dance all by myself!

Verse 5 says, you must ask and not doubt, because the one who doubts is like a waving sea. I asked God to explain to me this double-minded man. This is really a man of insanity! He is a crazy man. He really doesn't have good sense, doesn't know what he really looks like. He will fall on his knees and say, God make a way right now and soon as he gets up, he already says it's not going to work out. When he looks in the mirror, he doesn't even recognize himself!

I refuse to be a double minded man! I have to trust God! For God I live and for God I die! When I look in the mirror, I want to see God inside of me!

## God says, "I'm stretching your character!"

God wants to clean your facial expressions, to get your responses to where He wants them to be! We have to understand that the pressure that we're in is not designed to kill or destroy us, but it's designed to MAKE us. You're mad at God because it's not working out the way you want it to work out. God is working it for your good! There is some stuff inside of you that has to come out! Some evil stuff and some of it's just past weight. You're mad at somebody from the first grade, get over it, you're grown now!

God wants to bless you and set you free but you're holding onto your past and you're all upset. God is saying let it go so your character can come out now! When you see them, you have to be able to say brother it's alright, I forgive you and I let it go. I can't hold on to this anymore! It was just to make you better, to make you stronger!

So, you are in situations that will test your character, will you lie? I've heard people say it was just a white lie. Well tell a black one, a white one, a green one or blue one it's STILL a LIE!

# *Will you do the right thing when nobody is looking at you?*

I hate public bathrooms and I will go in there and God will say clean them up. I clean them because I have to obey what God says! I have to be a good steward over WHATEVER He tells me to be a steward over! If God tells me to make sure this is right, I have to make sure it's right WHEREVER I am.

Character is displayed in both VICTORY and DEFEAT. If you win you can still lift your hands up, but you don't have to flaunt around saying I'm the winner. You don't have to gloat. But even in defeat, character is still displayed! If you win or lose, let your character shine! Have a good attitude. We must always preserve our character.

> *"Your name will go farther than you will ever go; keep it clean."*
>
> -Poppa Joe

We have got to start handling things differently. In everything you have to exemplify Christ! A soft-spoken word will turn away wrath. (ref. Proverbs 15:1) I had to learn this. I had to learn how to suppress and hold down the old man and let the Holy Spirit reign.

We have to rely on the Holy Spirit more than our flesh. We want to respond from our flesh. Why? Because it feels good! You'll say, "well I just had to get that off my chest" but you look like a fool!

| **Character Killers** |
| --- |
| 1. Being self-centered |
| 2. Distorting the gospel to serve our own agenda |
| 3. Using your verbal skills to control others, intimidation. This is really a Jezebel spirit |
| 4. An appetite for power and possession |
| 5.  Corruption |

## *If you kill these in your life you will be better.*

One of the character builders is *righteousness.* Doing what is consistent with God's character. Live right! It's not always easy, you have to make some decisions and stand with them. Standing on God's word, people will walk away from you. God will bid you to stand and you're standing by yourself!

Another character builder is *godliness.* Have a lot of respect and reverence for God. Two things I'm scared of: the IRS and the Lord. I don't play with those two! You have to have faith. In the scripture it says, faith is the substance of things hoped for and the evidence of things not seen. (ref. Hebrews 11:1) I can't have faith if I don't have hope. You have to hope for something!

| **Character Builders** |
| --- |
| 1. Righteousness |
| 2. Godliness |
| 3. Self-sacrifice |
| 4. Patience |
| 5. Be gentle |

Some of you are in a bad place because you have no hope, so you can't believe God for anything. You've got to hope you're going to get out of the situations! Hope then changes to faith.

God taught me this some years ago when my father-in-law passed away. We went to the hospital, and I didn't know how to believe God. Sounds weird doesn't it? I didn't know how or what to believe. I just got a report and the situation was in front of us. The first thing God gave me was hope! Once I got hope, I started getting faith. But I never would have gotten faith, if I didn't have hope!

I started saying God you have to do it. I believe you can do it! The more the doctor told me there was a change in the situation we started believing in the hope and the faith to change the situation.

So, I must have hope, so I can have faith, to trust God! I also have to have a little character builder called *self-sacrifice* for God and others. What are you willing to sacrifice for others? A lot of us are selfish, we don't want to help anybody. We don't want to go the extra mile for anybody but guess what I realized? A lot of us want people to go the extra mile for us!

You will say, they didn't call me, and they knew I was sick. Then YOU call somebody! What are you willing to do for other people? Are you willing to walk that line for somebody else? It's so easy to walk the line for somebody we know, but that's not really the Lord!

How do you help a brother you don't even know? Hold his hand up, do what you can! We need some *patience.* In order to have character building you got to have some patience! You have to know how to endure some stuff!

The church has microwave faith, we're not used to waiting on anything. We have to know how to wait on the Lord! If you didn't get it right then, you just believed that God was going to do it. You didn't know how He was going to do it, you just believed that He would!

Have you ever seen the kind of grandmother that prays and walks the floor all night long saying Lord You have to do it! I don't know how, but You just got to do it! We saw a display of patience. I grew up in Uriah and my grandmother would feed the whole neighborhood. I got sick of taking hog meat down the road! The very ones that didn't like her, she fed them. The ones that would talk about her, I would be crying and saying why are you paying these people's light bill and she would say because that's the God thing to do!

I have folks come to me now and say, "it's because of your grandmother that I made it over, she taught us how to work!"

## *Wait on the Lord!*

Another thing that's going to help you build character is *being gentle.* You have to know how to be gentle! A controlled spirit that hates sin yet loves the sinner. Do you realize the way you talk can run people out the door? You may not like what they do, but you have to love the sinner! You have to learn how to embrace them.

Tell them that God loves them unconditionally. Well why do you say He loves us unconditionally? Because the bible says, when we were yet sinners Christ died for us. (ref. Romans 5:8) That means that nobody has it together!

A lot of us forgot that we were in a mess! We have forgotten that there were some things that we used to do and now, you don't have compassion for anybody. You don't have any self-control, you're all holy and you have run everyone from God. Now you don't know what to do because you thought you were doing the right thing. You don't know how to show any mercy. We MUST be gentle. God has put people in your hands, you either carry them or you crush them, the choice is yours!

Godly character does not occur as a result of individual transformation, but a result of primary development and nurturing. God is stretching us! Will you serve right? It's easy to obey God when it's something you WANT to do, but if God tells you to pack your house up and leave can you do that?

Can you trust God when He tells you to do something you really don't want to do? When He tells you to help somebody you really don't like. When God tells you to minster to somebody that doesn't believe like you do, will you still minster to them? Can you still show them love? Can you extend your hand and pull them out of their situation? The Bible says with love and kindness we draw; will you make yourself available?

God is trying to grow us up, to mature us. You have to go through this to mature! Monitor your responses! Don't just have diarrhea at the mouth anymore. Work on your facial expressions, this is a part of your character!

You love God but your face is all frowned up; looks like you have lemons in your mouth. Work on that! Work on the things you do when you're by yourself.  We want people to see God in us. If they can only see God by you SAYING, I'm pastor so and so or evangelist, you've missed it! The way you handle people when things are going bad shows your character!

We cannot walk in the spirit of offense. I had to learn and realize that when people come to me in love to help and change the situation, I can't get mad with them! Don't walk around in ignorance because you are in the spirit of offense. Everything we do and say is not the best way!

## *God wants to grow us up!*

Just like a Performance Evaluation, you can see what areas need improvement, where you can do better. God is not going to bless you in your ignorance. You don't know why you've done some things;

you just know that God said do it and then God will send somebody around you to show you why you did it.

Because you are studying this, best believe that they are going to try you. Who is they? The enemy! How are you going to respond to it? Now you know the word, you know how to respond, you should respond a little better this time. They may challenge you, but how will you respond to them? You may have the right answer, but make sure you give it back in love!  That is the key, LOVE!

You don't have to win every battle. Some battles aren't even worth winning at all! Know what to fight for and fight for the things that are important!   I wasn't an athlete, so I really don't care about winning, but you know what I do care about?   Finishing! I could come in dead last, but if I finish, I feel good about myself!

What's really important?! Is it winning so that you can say you came in first, or is it finishing with an understanding?! I want you to understand what God is doing and that God is trying to develop you. Don't be mad at the process anymore, get happy at the process!

God will truly work things out for you if you allow Him. He came to set some things straight, and because He is here, freedom is here! Don't miss this opportunity to get what God has for you! He knows better than anybody else what you need. For this reason, tell Him exactly what you're in need of!

## *Don't take small beginnings for granted!*

I think back to when we started. There were only about seven of us and we just had Bible study. This Bible study lasted maybe three years solid. However, we planted seeds and stood on God's word. Most people know what a revival and a conference is. But when we talk about seed service most of us don't understand the process of sowing seeds!

Background Scripture: Genesis 8: 22 KJV

> [22] While the earth remaineth, seedtime and harvest, and cold and heat, and summer and winter, and day and night shall not cease.

How many of you had a Big Momma or grand momma? What was one of the things that you would get at her house? Food! Then the Lord began to educate me on food. Big Momma didn't have a lot of money, but she always had food! The reason she always had food was because she always sowed food! You could always go to Big Momma's house and get something to eat in fifteen minutes! It didn't matter if there were fifteen people in her house or not, she always had food prepared.

I began to ask God why Big Momma only had food. He said, because she only SOWED food. There are some people who don't like to give and I'm not talking about money right now. The scripture above says, there will always be seed time and harvest time! How many of you want more from God? God wants to bless you but you're holding up your own blessings because you won't sow! We want more from God, but we won't sow!

Background Scripture: 1 John 2:16 KJV

> [16] For all that is in the world, the lust of the flesh, and the lust of the eyes, and the pride of life, is not of the Father, but is of the world.

Let me help you for a moment. This scripture is deeper than just being immoral. The lust of my eye, the lust of my flesh or the pride of life puts me in debt! God wants us to be set free and delivered and the enemy knows that! It is a commandment that God gave from the beginning of time. You won't sow therefore you won't reap!

There are two friends I want to introduce you to, SALE and CLEARANCE! They will always be around. These will get you in the store and as you walk pass or even to the section for the sale and clearance, the stuff they really want you to see is displayed.

We're talking about sow now and reap later! You're sowing for your future now! However, your current debt has you captive. Debt owns you, that's why you can't sow and reap the benefits of seed and harvest time!

How many of you have what I call "hit and miss blessings?" Things will go good for two or three months, then suddenly, all you worked for just falls down in six months. That's a representation of your sowing! If you start learning to sow through the good AND the bad, you will start reaping consistently through the good AND the bad!

Some of us won't give until we get our refund check and then we're not going to give anymore. What God is trying to do is set you up for a bigger blessing and it's based on what you set up in the earth!

Let's say you have a dime and a quarter, and they are seeds you are planting in a garden. You plant and cover them. But the job is not finished yet! We need to learn how to WORK in our gardens because if you don't watch your seed, weeds will take them out, weeds of discourse. You must also consider HOW you give! Giving worldly; when you give, you're already fussing. God wants a CHEERFUL giver! Don't give anymore until you get your heart right! If you have to fuss about giving, DON'T give!

I want to be a blessing to you and not a danger to you. How many pastors do you hear say don't give? Not very many! But I want you to get the full return on your giving!

God will take a dead seed and produce life out of it! If I take a dead seed, put it in the ground, cover it with dirt and I leave it there, it gets hard. But thank God for the Holy Spirit because He will water it! Thank God for the sun, the Son of man that brings out light and helps the seed break out through darkness and disappointment and come up producing!

You're planting for your future. You have to let God do the work in it and ask God to cultivate what God is doing! You're not the planter for real, you are just the one He allowed to drop it into the earth! It is not because your hand is so anointed, it is because of Him that allowed you to do it!

Plant a seed in the earth and before long, it breaks out the dirt. Say this out loud, "I'm planting for my future!" The seed grows. It gets bigger, and bigger and before I realize it, my future is over here now! I started out with nothing. The seed had no real substance or value, but God allowed me to reproduce for my future! It goes through stages and when it gets to maturity, I reap the benefits.

*You will not always see the results but know that it's working for your future!*

My challenge to you today is for a moment, allow yourself to be broke. Tell sale and clearance you're not friends anymore!  You have to sow because the more you sow the more you reap!  The more you give the more He gives back to you!  Pressed down shaken together and running over He will give unto you! (ref. Luke 6:38) But because you won't sow you don't reap!

Stop being a slave to debt. Debt is holding you captive! You want to do a thing and can't because debt is holding you. You have to start thinking like a king and queen! Stop buying cars and can't put gas in them, designer bags and don't even have a dollar in them. That doesn't make any sense!  We have to learn how to be good stewards. We must educate ourselves and learn how to sow seed into good ground! Some of this ground you're sowing in, is NOT good ground. That's why you can't get a return back. God wants us to be productive in the Kingdom, but we're so distracted by debt we can't do what He has called us to do!

## Sowing for your future! Sow NOW and reap LATER!

We say we love and believe God but won't even make a sacrifice to give. We will come up with all kinds of excuses as to why we can't give. God can't bless you while you're still holding on! If you don't have but 20 dollars and God says give it away, what is it going to do for you if you keep it?! Not much! But I guarantee you if you give it away now, God will allow somebody to come in and bless you! Your holding onto that little bit of nothing, is holding up the blessings God has for you! In this season you must trust God!

## *God wants to stretch you in your giving!*

You're anointed and can't even get to the program because you don't have gas money! We have to sow! I want everyone to be blessed, including myself! And I'm going to sow according to the leading of the Holy Spirit! I'm going to do it and trust God at His word!

God wants to bless us, but we have to know how to receive the blessing.  Operate in the anointing that God called you to! The scripture that says the poor will be with you always, I believe is not for broke people, but the poor in spirit, the poor in thinking.

I don't believe we are to walk in poverty and problems all our lives. I believe God has great things for the people of God in the earth. Now you can be like Big Momma and feed people when they come to your house, or you can start putting money in people's hands and watch God start putting money in your hands!

God has greater for us! You have to listen to what is being planted.

There is a release that God wants to give, there is anointing for it. God wants to set some things free in your life: financially, mentally, and the spirit says that if you just obey the word that is given to you, change will come your way!

## *Every time you sow you are sowing for your future!*

What you put out is what you get back! If something is happening or not happening in your life, don't get mad, change what your putting out! If you want people to be nice to you, be nice! If you want people to speak to you, speak!

Plant good seeds! But you don't want to plant any seeds, you just want to receive the blessings. Some of you like to receive but you don't like to give!  You have to change your mind frame. You are the righteousness of God! Abraham's seed! You are the King's sons and daughters and He makes provisions for you! Stop befriending sale and clearance! Find you another friend! Become friends with giving and you will be able to give again.

## *Because you GIVE, you are already blessed!*

I understand that some things are not for everybody.

Background Scripture: Psalm 75:6-7 KJV

> [6] For promotion cometh neither from the east, nor from the west, nor from the south. [7] But God is the judge: he putteth down one, and setteth up another.

Background Scripture: James 3:1 KJV

> [1] My brethren, be not many masters, knowing that we shall receive the greater condemnation.

I believe in the spirit that God is about to promote some people. And this promotion may not be on your job, but a promotion in the spirit. When I looked up the word promotion it said that it was just an elevation. God wants to elevate some people. There is about to be a promotion in the atmosphere. When you see promotion, it is God who promotes. That's even on your job, it's God that sets the promotion into place.

It is God who puts it on your supervisor's mind to be promoted. This is what you have to understand, the secular world is falling down because people of God won't accept the promotion at their secular job because they don't want the responsibility. So, what happens is, the person that is not saved, they will get the position because you won't apply for it.

People say, "I'll lose a friend if I do this". The devil is a liar, lose a friend or two. They'll say, "we have been working side by side for so long and I don't want to be over there." But you have been asking God to change some things. He wants to put you in a new position to make the change, but you won't apply for the job because you're scared of what the next person might say to you. So now the workplace is out of sync. Because you won't take the position. You won't step up and say, "I'll be the manager", or "I'll be the supervisor." But you'll let the person that sits next to you, who doesn't love anybody, who hates everybody, who doesn't care about anybody, get the position.

God told me to tell the saints to start applying! Listen to what He is telling you! He is trying to make a provision for you and your coworkers. God began to tell me that it is Him that sends forth the promotion. In the natural, they didn't want me to have the position. I told my boss one day that I don't want a position but that it's going to be God who is going to promote me. Every time they came to my desk about the job, I'd say it didn't matter! I'm content and I'm satisfied but it's in God's timing

Overlooked, and walked all over, but in the right season, God opened the door!  Let me help you in the spirit realm. God wants to promote you in the spirit! But you keep saying no! You just want to be a lay member. But God is saying, when I give you more. It is for you! Some of you want the promotion just for the check. But when you get the promotion, there are more responsibilities. When I was just a lay member, I didn't have as many responsibilities as when I became a deacon. But when I became a pastor, the responsibilities increased even more! Then God made me an overseer of a fellowship so now I don't just oversee one or two churches, but I oversee nine.

The reason I am pushing you is because when you will realize it, you will be sitting in the place that God wants you to be in. You were already doing the work before they gave you the job. You just had a title change.

With promotion comes responsibility. With responsibility comes accountability. Some of you just want to be promoted but you don't want the responsibility. What do I mean? The Bible says to whom much is given, much is required. (ref. Luke 12:48) And when much is required, much is given back to you. In the transition to your new place, God is calling you to more. It comes with the territory.

You must be accountable to some things. To your actions, to your ways, how you treat people because everybody is going to look at the manager. If I treat everybody badly, they will expect everyone under me to treat everybody badly. But if I hold the people under me up to a standard, and we become accountable one to another, then things work out.

I want to show you what the Lord showed me. Let's say you have a regular school music teacher. He is only responsible for his classroom. Then God elevates them to lead teacher. So now they are not just over their classroom, but they have to manage the whole music department which includes 3 other teachers.

Their title changed, so the responsibilities changed. Therefore, they are held to a higher accountability than when they were just the music teacher. Now if something goes wrong in one of the other classrooms, people are coming to the music department head. They want to know what's going on in the department and how will it be fixed. The lead teacher has to work with all the other teachers in the department and if they are not capable, they will be replaced! It works the same in the spirit!

## *With promotion comes more responsibility and more accountability!*

That music teacher is was promoted to lead teacher and now to the assistant principal. From assistant principal they go to being principal. Now they oversee the janitor, the cafeteria workers, the bus drivers, the librarian, every lead teacher, every teacher and the students. More responsibility. Every promotion is added responsibility.

They get promoted from principal to the superintendent. They have several schools in the county. Now they oversee the school, every principal, every teacher, every bus driver, every cafeteria worker, every reading and math specialist, because they have been promoted. They have to walk in a different standard now because not only are the principals looking up the them, but they also set the tone for the whole county as it relates to education. This is the kind of promotion that God wants to do in the spirit.

Everybody is not just a pew member. God is calling you out of the pews to do the work. And every time God calls you out of the pews to do the work, He gives you more responsibilities. There is a woman at my church that used to just be on the dance team. Now she is over the whole dance ministry and through conversation she told me that she has to live holy now because the children and the other dancers are looking up to her. There are some things she just can't do anymore.

The Lord told me to tell you that with the title comes responsibilities. I believe in works before titles! You will be doing the work before the title falls into place. If nobody ever calls me apostle, that's ok because I've been DOING the work for a long time!  Now when you see people asking for the title really quickly and there is no work behind them, they are probably out of order!

In the spirit, God is elevating us from place to place. As a leader there are some things that you can't do anymore. I can't even have a conversation the way I used to have because the Holy Spirit checks me on some things. I can't live a certain way because I am leader. God says, if you are a leader, you will be judged harsher than the ones that aren't leaders.

In the board of education if the county starts to sink, they look at the superintendent.  I hear God saying that I want to promote you, but the reason why the promotion is not coming the way you want it to come is because your heart is not right! I can't let you lead anyone, and you have contamination inside you. Then God says I trust you to be a leader because your heart is right. Now it's time for the promotion but there are some things in you that need to come out.

Some of you are in a birthing stage right now and you don't even realize it. There is a leaping on the inside of you and you are rebelling against it and God is saying I'm moving you to the next place! I'm girding you up. I have searched you and your heart is right!  It will be just like when Samuel went to Jesse's house and asked if he had any sons and to line them up. Jesse had a lot of sons, some of them

LOOKED good, some sounded good. Some cute, some big, some strong, but then he had one that he didn't even bring into line up. His resume wasn't even on the desk!

There are some people whose resume was overlooked but they still got the job. Some people didn't even apply for the job and they got the job!  Don't know how you got it, they just called you! All the boys were in front of Jesse and he'd walk by and the Lord would say, that's not him!  He got through all the sons in the line and he asked Jesse if he had anymore sons! Jesse told him he had one in the field, watching the sheep. That's why David says the Lord is my shepherd and I shall not want!

Jesse said he had one more son, but he didn't look good. The Bible says that he was rugged! And Samuel told him to go and get him. When he saw him God said, that's the one! (ref 1 Samuel 16) As I was riding up the highway one day God said, "the reason why David was the one, was because his heart was right!" The Bible declares him as a man after God's own heart!  Sometimes you will feel bad before you get the position.  God was already preparing David to be king and he didn't even realize it!

Promotion is taking place now! There are callings that are being birthed inside of you right now and God is requiring you to do more. There's a brand-new level of responsibility and you have to learn how to be responsible. You have to learn how to be accountable! Are you dependable; can God depend on you? Come rain or shine can God depend on you? When things get bad, will your hands still be lifted up to Him? He just wants to know if He can depend on you!

God is promoting things right now! It is God who sends forth a promotion. He tells Jeremiah, "I knew you already in your mother's womb. I had already ordained you in your mother's womb. Now you have to walk it out for your promotion" (ref Jeremiah 1) You have to move now! There are people waiting on you to get up! Stop looking at your current position! God is saying it's not meant for you to stay in that place!  That's why He has been challenging you with more duties and responsibilities. He has to get your heart right for the next place.

The Bible says, "I give you pastors after my own heart." (ref. Jeremiah 3:15) That's why everybody can't be a pastor, you have to be compassionate towards people. You will have people telling you you're crazy, they wouldn't take this or that, but as the pastor you have to go!

God knows how to set you up to get you to where He wants you to be!  God is setting you up for your next place!

# *It's a set up!*

From rags to riches! If you stay faithful to God! God knows the heart of the man! The heart has got to be right for the promotion. The mouth speaks from the heart! I used to be just a regular programmer. Then I went to a program analyst. Then senior programmer. It came with a bigger office and nice furniture. That's why my desk is dirty now because I have more responsibilities! But understand this, I was already doing the work before the title.  You're going to be just like Joshua and wake up one day and you're leading the whole tribe! You must learn how to get yourself in position!

## *To whom much is given, much is required!*

I keep asking God what more can I give. And He keeps saying there is more inside of me than what I can see! He says the same about you! There is so much more for us to do! Do I get tired? Yes! But I thank God for what He has given me, for the responsibilities He has entrusted to me! Keep doing the work! Get ready for the promotion!

You had to go through it to appreciate it. It's more valuable to you now! I hope you read something that will brighten up your day and a seed was planted that will make you think and act on what God has called you to do!

## *I don't know what God is about to do but we MUST be ready! We can't get weary in the process!*

Prayer:

*God, we thank You and we bless Your name. We give You glory. We give You honor. We thank You for the word Lord God, the word on the season of stretching. You are stretching our character, our obedience in You, Lord God! If there is anything in our hearts that we are holding on to that is stopping our character from being developed in the right way, right now, deliver us from it in the name of Jesus! We are going to lay it at Your feet! We lay it at the altar right now and say Lord take it out of our heart!*

*Sometimes our flesh wants to take over and take control, help us now! God we just need clarity in this process. Help us to develop our faith, our patience, our perseverance, to go through this the right way! Help us to be gentle so that we deal with people the right way. Help us Jesus! God we just thank You now for the movement of Your Holy Spirit that is resting within us. We thank You for what You're doing, though it doesn't feel good in this process of being stretched. We get weary, we want to give up, but send some hope our way! And when You send the hope, faith will come behind it soon! God, we give You glory, and we give You honor.  In the name of Jesus, we pray!*

*~Amen!*

## EARLY LIFE, MARRIAGE, CHILDREN, AND FULL TIME JOB

Joseph Dean, IV is the oldest of three children born to Joseph and Larphillis Dean. He grew up in a home where his parents believed in working hard, but most of all serving God with a sincere heart. Joseph accepted Christ as his Savior at an early age and followed the rules of his parents, "serve God with a sincere heart". His parents knew that he was different because of various experiences he encountered, even to the point whereas he thought he was losing his mind. Nevertheless, he was not losing his mind; God was preparing him for the role of being a chosen leader to lead the people.

Joseph surrendered to the ministry early in his young-adulthood. After graduating in 1994 from J. U. Blacksher High School in Uriah, AL, Joseph attended Talladega College in Talladega, AL. His major was Computer Science with a minor in Mathematics. In 1998, during his senior year at Talladega College, God worked in a mysterious way by allowing the Holy Spirit to manifest and birth a vision within him to start Lighthouse Ministries. What a life changing experience! God knew the plans for Joseph's life which is why he blessed him with a woman of worth, Schmieka (Davis) Dean. They were united as one on May 19, 2001. As of 2018, they are blessed with two children, Ashtun, born October 27, 2005 and Hannah, born June 3, 2016. Joseph is currently employed full-time with the State of Alabama in the Transportation Department as the Web Team Supervisor.

Joseph successfully completed the Alabama Department of Transportation Leadership Academy in 2017.  This Academy is limited to the numbers of employees selected; however, because of his leadership ability, potentials, and skills to make a difference, he received the opportunity to partake in a great opportunity.

## MINISTRY AND ACCOMPLISHMENTS

"And the LORD answered me, and said, Write the vision, and make it plain upon tables, that he may run that readeth it.".  Habakkuk 2:2 KJV

God planted a seed that opened doors and continues to open doors of opportunities.  Joseph received his license to preach God's Word on May 2, 1999 by Rev. Kenneth W. Kidd and the Mt. Triumph Missionary Baptist Church of Uriah, Alabama.  He was later ordained on June 16, 2002, by Rev. T. L. Douglas and the Grove Hill Missionary Baptist Church of Uriah, AL.  He and Schmieka started an Empowerment Worship held locally and they traveled to other counties as well sharing this life changing experience.  As time progressed, Bible Study was organized and held on Mondays at Joseph & Schmieka' s home in the living room on West Cypress Court in Montgomery, AL with only six (6) people in 2007.  Joseph never stopped going far and near to reach the lost souls because he understands the assignment God has ordained and appointed him to do. His wife, son, and daughter are major role players because through their love and support, going back and forth makes it easier for Joseph to continue the vision God gave him.

In 2008, Lighthouse Ministries began church services every month on the first (1st) Sunday. Things began to venture out even the more because in 2009, services were implemented on third (3rd) Sundays. All of these services were held on the patio in their home. Also, in 2009, they held the first (1st) baptismal service for several people. During the holiday season, the first (1st) Christmas dinner and first (1st) Watch Night service was held to remember Christ's birth.

In 2010, God allowed greater opportunities to arise! Joseph opened the doors for all of the members and partners affiliated with Lighthouse Ministries to participate at will in a corporate fast; and through this great sacrifice as a whole body, the ministry was able to purchase two (2) vans in cash, acquired sound equipment by donations, developed the children's ministry and experienced the Day of Pentecost. From this point on, the ministry has been growing yearly.

In 2014, the first (1st) Combined Youth Explosion was held which included over seven (7) different ministries. There were over one hundred (100) youth in attendance. Also, during this year, the very first (1st) Women's Conference was held which attracted over one hundred fifty (150) women and men. The praise and worship team grew in numbers. The very first combined choir was organized. There were over twenty-five (25) individuals that transferred membership from other ministries or joined via baptism. Overall, two hundred (200) visitors graced this ministry with their presence and spiritual experiences.

In 2015, the growth of individuals from seven (7) people in the living room on West Cypress Court grew to over fifty-five (55) people.  During this growth, the people served God in the living room, the patio, the movie theater, now currently a store front.  God is preparing Joseph and his flock for a greater location so they can be that light to stand on a hill.

In 2016, God expanded the vision.  Joseph was officially ordained as an Apostle on Sunday, October 23, 2016.  He currently serves as the senior pastor of Lighthouse Ministries in Montgomery, Alabama, St. Paul Baptist Church in Uriah, AL, and presiding prelate of Lighthouse International Fellowship – A Kingdom Agenda.

Prior to being officially affirmed as an Apostle, Joseph has (10) different ministries that work as one through Lighthouse International Fellowship, Inc.  LIF was established in 2015 and the first official board meeting was held with all leaders November 7, 2015.  Under LIF, there were three (3) combined ministry launches held in 2016 during February, April, and May.  These launches were held to educate all individuals about the importance of working together.  The scripture for LIF comes from I Corinthians 12:20-25 because it takes every part of the body to work as one for Christ.

He was most recently honored as a Distinguished Pastor of Alabama by the Tuskegee United Women's League, INC.

## BEING A SERVANT

- Opened home to stranger(s) on multiple occasions
- Worked with the local Salvation Army on several occasions to deliver food for the needy
- Opened the Clothes Closet through Lighthouse Ministries to provide clothing for families that fall into hardships
- Assisted families with utility bills, relocation, finding employment, and resume creations
- Tutored high school students in mathematics

www.ingramcontent.com/pod-product-compliance
Lightning Source LLC
Chambersburg PA
CBHW051232250726
48655CB00006B/2732